GU
GULL

Welcome to Gumtree Gully. It's a place where animals like Bluey the Possum and Rocky the Wallaby live and play with their friends. But it's also a place where danger is lurking just around the corner. As you read the adventures of Bluey and Rocky and their friends in Gumtree Gully, you'll find some lessons hidden inside the story about God and Jesus and us. Watch out for the section at the end of each chapter that tells you 'What's inside this story'.

I hope you enjoy it.

KEL RICHARDS

Gumtree Gully

Matthias Media
(St Matthias Press Ltd ACN 067 558 365)
Email: info@matthiasmedia.com.au
Internet: www.matthiasmedia.com.au
Please visit our website for current postal and telephone contact information.

Matthias Media (USA)
Email: sales@matthiasmedia.com
Internet: www.matthiasmedia.com
Please visit our website for current postal and telephone contact information.

ISBN 978 1 921068 11 9

Cover and internal illustrations by Graham Wade.
Design and typesetting by Lankshear Design.

Contents

matthiasmedia
SYDNEY · YOUNGSTOWN

1. The Ranger

BLUEY THE POSSUM and Rocky the Wallaby were playing a game. They were racing between two big gum trees, each trying to prove that he was faster than the other.

Rocky would lean forward and hop on his powerful hind legs in huge strides, while Bluey ran overhead, leaping from branch to branch in the tall river red gum trees. Each time they raced, the result was a dead heat —Bluey was just as fast through the trees as Rocky was over the ground.

Three times they raced, and three times they got exactly the same result. After the third race, the two young friends went and sat in the shade, with their backs against the trunk of the biggest gum tree.

"Why do they call you Bluey?" asked Rocky.

"Because I've got red fur", said the possum.

"That makes no sense."

"You've got to understand", Bluey explained, "that Australians call most red-heads 'Bluey'. I think it's meant to be a joke."

"In that case, I don't get it", said Rocky. "Come on, let's race again."

And for a fourth time, the two raced over the course, and, for the fourth time, the result was exactly the same —a dead heat—a tie between the hopping rock wallaby and the leaping possum.

While they were catching their breath, Bluey the Possum suddenly said, "Ssshh! I think I can hear something…"

"What can you hear?" asked Rocky.

"Nothing at all when you're talking. Now keep quiet and listen very carefully."

Both animals pricked up their ears and listened very carefully. Then they heard it: the sound of big, heavy boots, crunching over the dead leaves.

"Someone's coming", said Bluey in a hushed voice.

"I wonder," said Rocky, "I wonder if it could be…"

His voice trailed away. Both young animals knew they were thinking of the same person. But it was Bluey who whispered, "Could it be… the Ranger?"

"You go and look", insisted Rocky. "From the tree-tops you should be able to see."

Bluey hesitated only for a moment. Then he took off, climbing straight up the tree trunk to the very top, then leaping from branch to branch until he reached a point near the top of one of the tallest gum trees where he could see the track that led into Gumtree Gully.

Down below on the track, walking into the gully, he saw a man. The man was wearing the big, heavy boots, the wide-brimmed hat, and the khaki uniform of the Wildlife Ranger.

A minute later, Bluey was back by Rocky's side, saying breathlessly, "It's him! It's him! It's the Ranger!"

Rocky looked worried. He said, "What do you think he wants? Will he give us orders? Will he want us to clean up Gumtree Gully for him? Do you think he might pack us up and move us somewhere else?"

"Let's ask the others", Bluey suggested. "They've lived here longer than us. They'll know about the Ranger."

The first one they asked was Curly the Koala. They found him curled up in one of the forks of his favourite blue gum, sound asleep. Bluey had to shake his grey, furry shoulder to wake him up. When they finally got him to understand that the Ranger was coming, Curly said, "I don't care. I just want to sleep. Go away and let me snooze, there's good kids."

Next they went to where Jacko the Kookaburra was sitting, on a higher branch of the same tree. When they told Jacko about the Ranger, he burst out laughing.

"What a joke!" he said. "As if we should bother to take the Ranger seriously! I think this idea about the Ranger being important is a real hoot! I don't care what the Ranger thinks or what the Ranger says. I just treat him as great big joke!" And he began to laugh his feathery head off.

On the ground, under the same gum tree, Rocky and Bluey found Sneaky the Goanna. When they told him the news, he said, "So, he's coming, is he? I think I'll hide. I suggest you do the same. Don't let the Ranger catch you and start giving you orders. Duck out of the way. If he happens to see you, agree with whatever he says and then ignore him as soon as he goes away again. That's what I do."

Rocky and Bluey weren't happy with any of these suggestions. They headed towards the creek. There they found Paddle the Platypus having a swim. He was swimming slowly and gracefully, doing backstroke and heading upstream. They called him over to the bank and told him the news.

"So, the Ranger's coming, is he?" said Paddle. "All I can say is—bother! What a nuisance! I don't want the Ranger telling me what to do—giving me jobs to do. I just want to play and swim and frolic in the water. That's what life is all about—having fun. Bother the Ranger! That's what I say."

And he dived back into the creek. At that moment, Wise Old Wombat waddled out of his hole in the creek bank. Rocky and Bluey told him about the Ranger.

Wombat thought for a moment and then sat the two young animals down and told them a story.

"The Ranger", said Wombat, "has the right to expect us to listen to him and obey him. You see, the Ranger is

also a farmer. This land—Gumtree Gully—is on his farm. He paid for it, so he owns it. When he first bought it, this gully was barren and lifeless—it had been cleared and felled. He paid for all the trees and bushes and plants you see around us. He planted them with his own hands. This is all his work.

"As for us animals who live here… well, you were probably too young at the time to remember it, but he rescued each and every one of us from dangerous places where the bush was dying, and brought us here to live in safety and peace. We owe our lives to him. Because of his loving care, the government appointed him Wildlife Ranger to look after Gumtree Gully and to look after us. So, when the Ranger comes, you listen to him carefully and do whatever he tells you to do."

What's inside this story?

The Ranger in this story is a bit like God in our world. God made this world and everything in it—including us. Just like the Ranger, God brought us into this world he created, so that we could live here and serve him.

This means God is in charge of this world—he is the King.

God is not a bossy, selfish king, like some human kings. He's kind and loving and good. That's why the world he's made is full of good things—just like the beautiful gully the Ranger planted, which was full of gum trees, bushes and wildflowers.

God makes people, too, and gives us life. This means he's *our* king. We should *read* what God says in the Bible and *do* what he says, just like the animals of Gumtree Gully should *listen* carefully to the Ranger and *do* whatever he tells them to do.

God made this world, and he speaks to this world through his one and only Son, Jesus Christ. God appointed Jesus to be the Ruler—the King—of this world, just like the government appointed the farmer to be the Wildlife Ranger to care for Gumtree Gully, putting him in charge of the gully and the animals in it.

Understanding that we have been made, loved and cared for should make us appreciate what God has done.

The Bible says:

> Our Lord and God, you are worthy to receive glory, honour and power, because you created all things, and by your decision they came to be. (REVELATION 4:11)

> In the beginning, God created the heavens and the earth. (GENESIS 1:1)

2. The animals

DEAD LEAVES COULD BE heard crunching under the heavy boots of the Ranger as he came over the rise and walked down the track into Gumtree Gully. The Ranger was a friendly-looking man—tall, bearded and sun-tanned. But many of the animals who lived in the gully were frightened of him.

As his shadow passed over the creek bank, Paddle the Platypus dived into the underwater entrance to his hole in the side of the creek, leaving behind a slow-spreading ripple on the surface of the water. Jacko the Kookaburra flew away with a flutter of feathery wings, landing on top of a distant gum tree.

Curly the Koala seemed to sleep on undisturbed, yet he curled himself up into an even tighter ball in the fork of the tree where he slept, trying to look as small as possible so he wouldn't be noticed.

Sneaky the Goanna scuttled underneath an over-hanging slab of rock, pulling his long tail in after him. Then he kept very still. Even Wise Old Wombat was a bit nervous about this tall, important person who was now striding through their gully. So he waddled back into the warm darkness of his wombat hole.

Only the two youngest animals, Rocky the Wallaby and Bluey the Possum, were unsure of what to do. At first they thought they might hide behind one of the river red gums, but bits of them kept sticking out.

"Pull in that long tail of yours!" snapped Bluey to Rocky. "It's sticking way out into the track. The Ranger will see it the minute he gets here."

"Well, what about that bushy tail of *yours*?" complained Rocky. "Anyone with half an eye will be able to see that. Can't you tuck it up behind you out of sight?"

"Oh, this isn't working", moaned Bluey. "We'd better find somewhere else to hide."

Rocky the Wallaby tried hopping up to the rocks of the overhanging cliff above the gully, but there wasn't a rock big enough to hide behind. At last he found a hollow tree stump that had been burnt out in a bushfire many years before. He squeezed himself into the hollow space but, once again, his long tail kept hanging out behind him, giving away his hiding place.

Bluey the Possum climbed up the tallest tree he could find, nervously leaping from branch to branch as the Ranger drew closer and closer. Finally, way up high, near the thinnest branch at the very top, he stopped, clung on and kept very still.

From his perch, Bluey saw the Ranger walk into the

clearing in the bush below. The Ranger stood in the middle of the clearing, took off his wide-brimmed hat and scratched his head. Then he gave a friendly laugh and said, "Come on out, all of you. I know you're all trying to hide so you might as well come out."

Just then, the thin branch Bluey was clinging to gave way under his weight, snapping with a crack and sending the possum tumbling down through the gum leaves.

Fortunately, Bluey grabbed a branch as he flew past. His sharp little claws dug into it and held him safe, while the leaves he had knocked off went fluttering to the ground.

"Ah, there you are, Bluey", said the Ranger, looking up. Sheepishly Bluey crept down to the ground and stood at the Ranger's feet. The Ranger glanced over at the hollow tree stump and called out, "I think the owner of that long, grey tail should come out of his hiding place".

The tail flopped about for a moment or two, and then Rocky the Wallaby appeared with a silly grin on his face. He joined Bluey in the clearing, sitting at the Ranger's feet.

Once again Ranger looked up and called out, "Curly, I know you're only pretending to be asleep. Come down here and join our group. And Jacko—you're not far enough away to be out of sight, so you might as well join us too."

Just then Wise Old Wombat waddled out of his hole, muttering, "I know I was foolish to hide, so here I am".

"Thank you, Wombat, very wise", said the Ranger. "Now Sneaky, I can see the tip of your black and yellow tail, so you might as well give up your hiding place under that rock. And Paddle, you always hide in the same place—in your creek bank home—so you can come out and join us too."

A few minutes later, all the animals of Gumtree Gully had gathered in the clearing and were sitting around the Ranger. He sat down on the stump of a long-dead tree and said, "Now, you animals know that I gave you just one rule that you must obey. Can any of you tell me what that rule was?"

Each animal looked around at all the others until Wombat cleared his throat and said, "Um, I think the only rule you gave us was that we must clear away the dead leaves. You said we should rake up all the leaf litter into a clearing—a safe place well away from the bush."

"And why did I tell you this?" asked the Ranger.

"Because…" began Bluey and then he stopped, feeling foolish.

"Go on Bluey", said the Ranger in a kind voice.

"Because", continued Bluey, "because leaf litter is a fire hazard".

"That's right", said the Ranger. "Leaf litter is a fire hazard. A bushfire could completely destroy Gumtree Gully. Worse than that, a bushfire could kill every animal here. That's true, isn't it?"

All the animals nodded in agreement.

"That's why I've told you that the one job you must do for me is to clear away the leaf litter—rake up all the dead leaves into a pile in a clearing near the creek where they won't be a fire risk. I gave you this instruction for your own good."

There was a long pause while the Ranger looked around at the faces of the animals gathered about the clearing.

"So, then", he resumed, "why have none of you done this? As I walked down the track today, I could see dead leaves everywhere. I could hear dead leaves crunching under my boots. There are dead leaves piled up thickly around many tree trunks. You haven't been following my orders, have you?"

He spoke sternly. Each animal hung its little head and looked embarrassed.

"I'm going again now", said the Ranger. "I'm leaving the gully for you animals to look after. There is only one rule for you to obey: clear up the leaf litter. Get rid of the dead leaves and keep the gully safe from fire. That is my only instruction. Will you all obey it this time?"

Every animal sheepishly nodded its head. With that, the Ranger got up and left.

As soon as he was gone, all the animals started talking.

"Well," said Curly with a yawn, "the rest of you should get on with clearing up the leaf litter. I have some sleep to catch up on."

"Aren't you going to help?" asked Bluey.

"Help?" muttered Curly. "Yes, of course I'll help. But later. Not now—later. After I've had a sleep." And he lumbered lazily back up into his tree.

"Well I'm not helping", hooted Jacko the Kookaburra. "I think it's a bit of a joke. The idea that we animals should clear up the gully and keep it clean is hysterically funny. I could burst my sides laughing at the whole idea. So the rest of you can do it, if you like, while I sit on my branch and have a chuckle about it."

Sneaky the Goanna said, "Well, I won't be clearing up any leaf litter. No-one tells me what to do—not even the Ranger. I run my life my own way, thank you very much. This little goanna doesn't take orders from anyone."

"But—but—", stuttered Rocky, "I saw you nod your head. You seemed to agree with the clean-up when the Ranger was here."

"Well, I was lying then, wasn't I?" snapped Sneaky, and he hurried away to find a place in the sun.

Rocky and Bluey turned to the two remaining animals, Paddle and Wombat, and asked them if they would help clean up the leaf litter.

"The purpose of life is pleasure", said Paddle as he waddled off towards the creek. "I'm here to have fun—to swim and to splash about. Doing the Ranger's work would spoil my fun, so I'm out."

Wombat said, "I will most certainly help to clean up the dead leaves and all the leaf litter. I want to obey the Ranger's instructions and I want the gully to be safe from bushfire. But I have some important things to attend to in my wombat hole—I'm in the middle of painting the walls of the tunnels. As soon as I've done that, I'll be back out to help with the clean up. In the meantime, you two young animals can make a start."

As the brown, furry bottom of Wombat disappeared down his burrow, Rocky and Bluey looked at each other. Rocky said, "Let's make a start cleaning up the leaf litter tomorrow. What do you say?"

"Yes", said Bluey. "Tomorrow—that's a good idea."

With that, the two young friends ran off into the bush to play.

What's inside this story?

In their different ways, all the animals said "No" to the Ranger. They rejected his rule and the order he had given them to obey—an order that was for their own good.

In just the same way, we all say "No" to God. We reject him from being king over us. We try to be our own king instead. Even though God is the *true* King, we don't want him to be *our* king. We do what *we* want to do, instead of what God wants us to do. We pretend that *we* are king instead of God.

This causes lots of problems.

By trying to do things our own way and ignoring God's rules, we hurt each other and make a big mess of God's good world. Just like the animals who left a big mess in Gumtree Gully and made it a dangerous place to live by leaving lots of leaf litter lying about.

The Bible says:

> All of us have sinned and fallen short of God's glory. (Romans 3:23)
>
> No-one is acceptable to God. No-one understands or searches for God. They have all turned away. (Romans 3:10-12)

3. The bushfire

IT WAS A BLAZING HOT summer's day in Gumtree Gully. Early in the morning the two youngest animals, Rocky the Wallaby and Bluey the Possum, had been playing among the bushes and the wildflowers. But as the day got hotter, they went down to a cool spot by the creek to lie in the shade and listen to the water splashing over the rocks.

Paddle the Platypus swam up to them and said, "This is where you two ought to be on a hot day—here in the water with me. It's very cool and refreshing in here."

"No thanks", said Bluey. "I can't swim."

Paddle snorted. "Oh, come on! Swimming's easy. It just comes naturally to me. What about you, Rocky? I suppose you're going to tell me that you can't swim either?"

"That's right", said Rocky. "I can't swim either."

"But it's so easy", said Paddle as he swam in a lazy backstroke across to the other side of the creek and back again. "Come on in and give it a try."

"I'll tell you what", said Bluey, "I'll come into the water with you and try to swim if you'll climb up one of those tall gum trees with me. So, how about it?"

"Not on your nelly!" snapped Paddle. "I might fall off a branch and land right on my noggin. I'd do myself some damage. That would be very silly."

"It's about as silly as me trying to swim", said Bluey with a laugh.

At that, the platypus dived under the water and swam away, leaving a trail of tiny bubbles on the surface of the creek.

As the morning wore on, all the animals became sleepy. They lay down in the shade to doze through the hottest part of the day. While they were sleeping, dark clouds began to pile up in the sky—big black clouds building up like floating mountains above the gully.

A sudden loud crash of thunder woke all the animals.

"What was that?" said Bluey, rubbing his eyes.

"Was it an explosion?" asked Rocky.

"It sounded like a small war!" said Sneaky the Goanna, coming out from underneath a rock.

"It even woke me up!" complained Curly the Koala.

"You people look so startled and silly!" laughed Jacko the Kookaburra. "You're quite a hoot, the lot of you."

Just then the thunder crashed again. Wise Old Wombat put his hairy nose out of his wombat hole and said, "Looks like we're in for a summer storm".

"What's a summer storm?" asked Bluey.

"The worst kind", muttered Wombat, turning around and disappearing into his hole again.

The black clouds were not directly overhead. The

animals on the creek bank watched as the dark storm circled around them—from the south, to the west, then drifting towards the north.

Inside those clouds were sudden flashes. After each flash, there was a loud crash of thunder. Then a giant spark of lightning shot from one cloud to another. The roar was deafening.

"Rocky, I don't think I like this", said Bluey in a small voice. "I wish it would go away."

"It will, it will", said Sneaky the Goanna. "It always does."

But just then another brilliant white flash of lightning shot out of the blackest cloud and struck the ground somewhere over the treetops at the far end of Gumtree Gully.

The thunder that came with the lightning strike seemed to make the ground tremble. Then the wind sprang up and the clouds were blown further and further away. In the distance they could be seen releasing their rain in a heavy downpour. But none of that rain fell into Gumtree Gully.

Bluey the Possum scampered up to the top of a tall river red gum and looked about. The wind was stronger now and the summer storm was far away on the horizon. Then Bluey sniffed the breeze and smelled something that he didn't like.

"Smoke!" he yelled out to the animals in the clearing below. "I can smell smoke!"

"I'll take a look", called out Jacko as he spread his wings and took off over the trees.

Bluey ran back down the tree trunk and joined the other animals in the clearing, waiting for the kookaburra to return. They waited one minute.

Then two.

Then three.

And then Jacko flew back and landed in the clearing. This time even Jacko wasn't laughing.

"It's a bushfire," he gasped, "burning at the far end of Gumtree Gully".

"Perhaps it will burn itself out", said Curly the Koala hopefully.

"Perhaps it will stay at the far end of the gully, away

from us", said Rocky.

"But perhaps it won't", said Bluey worriedly. "Then what do we do?"

"Stay near the creek", said the Wise Old Wombat who had just come out of his burrow. "That's all we can do."

The youngest animals hurried over to Wombat's side. They said, "It will be all right, won't it Wombat?"

Instead of answering, Wombat looked anxious and said, "You sometimes call me 'wise', young animals. The problem is, I'm not wise enough. In fact, right now, I feel very foolish. We have not obeyed the Ranger's orders. None of us have. And there is leaf litter scattered all over Gumtree Gully. There are piles of dead leaves surrounding many of the trees. This whole gully is a firetrap—all because we did not obey the Ranger's order to clear up the leaf litter. And now it's too late. Now the fire has started and all those dry, dead leaves will be fuel for the fire to burn."

Wombat shook his head slowly and sadly. Above them, a great cloud of smoke curled its way up into the sky. A short while later, they could see the flames—huge, red flames—leaping high into the air. The wind was getting stronger all the time, whipping around them and pushing the fire from tree to tree—from bush to bush—until the ridge-tops on every side were burning. The temperature rose and the air was filled with a stinging, stabbing heat, hotter than the midday sun.

Gumtree Gully was surrounded by flames. And the animals knew that they were in deadly danger.

What's inside this story?

The animals of Gumtree Gully have brought this disaster on themselves. They are paying the price for not obeying the Ranger. They all said "No" to him—not just with their voices but with their actions too. They ignored him and they ignored his orders. They did not do what he told them to do.

It's just like us and God.

God is the only true King. He won't let people go on saying "No" to him. He will do something about it. The punishment for saying "No" to God is not a bushfire; it's being shut out of God's kingdom and God's family forever.

By our actions, we say "No" to God. We ignore him and refuse to obey him. Because we *all* do that, we *all* end up hurting each other and making a mess of God's world.

But God won't let us go on saying "No" to him. He won't let us go on pretending to be kings, ignoring his orders and running our lives without him. One day God will show everyone that *he* is the one *true* King. He will set up a wonderful kingdom that will never end. And on that day, everyone who has been saying "No" to him will be shut out of his kingdom forever.

The Bible says:

> We will all die once, and then face judgement.
>
> (Hebrews 9:27)

4. The rescue

A TERRIFYING BUSHFIRE was burning through Gumtree Gully. Every ridge surrounding the gully was alight, flames licking up the bush on all sides. The gully was cut off. The animals huddled in a clearing in the middle beside the creek, afraid to move and not sure what they should do.

"Listen to that roar!" said Bluey the Possum, trembling, his eyes wide with terror.

His young friend, Rocky the Wallaby, said, "I never knew that a bushfire made so much noise".

At that moment, Jacko the Kookaburra flew back into the clearing and said, "I've had a look around and the flames are getting higher—they're leaping from treetop to treetop and they should be here before long".

Sneaky the Goanna began to panic, running back and forth, shouting, "What can we do? What can we do?" He stuck his head under a pile of dead leaves so that he couldn't see the approaching flames.

Wise Old Wombat shook his head and said, "I don't feel very wise now. I don't know what to do."

Even sleepy old Curly the Koala was wide awake and

very worried. "But there must be something we can do", he kept saying. "There must be something!"

"Well, I'm staying here in the creek", said Paddle the Platypus. "The creek will keep me safe."

"And I'm flying off", said Jacko. "Sorry to leave you blokes in such a pickle but I'm not staying here to be burned to death by the bushfire."

With those words, he spread his large, feathery wings and took off. But, by now, thick clouds of grey smoke were filling the whole of Gumtree Gully. In the thick, grey smoke Jacko lost his way and flew smack into the trunk of a tall river red gum. Feathers were knocked off the end of his wing and his wing muscles were bruised with the impact.

Trying again, he crashed heavily to the ground, one wing dragging behind him. With only one wing still working, Jacko flew around in circles in the dense smoke for several minutes before landing and then limping back into the clearing by the creek.

Wise Old Wombat examined the wing and said helpfully, “Those feathers will re-grow in a week or two, Jacko. Long before then, your wing muscles will heal. Don’t worry. You should be able to fly again in no time.”

“What are you talking about, silly old Wombat?” squawked Jacko. “What do you mean, ‘In a week or two’? Long before then I’ll be dead. Have you forgotten about the bushfire?”

But the animals of Gumtree Gully were not the only ones who knew about the bushfire.

From his homestead, the Ranger saw the smoke and sprang into action. Throwing some old sugar bags into the back of his truck, he drove to the point where the walking track into the gully began. Here, he stopped to soak the sugar bags in the creek water. After draping the wet bags over his head and shoulders, he ran at the wall of flames blocking the track into the gully.

The Ranger leapt over burning grass, dodged burning trees and kept running. He ran through the blackened stumps of gum trees. Burning cinders drifted through the air and settled on his arms, legs, hair and clothes. He brushed them off and kept on running, but each time he did so, he got burned.

In the thick smoke, the Ranger stumbled into rocks and bushes which bruised him and scratched him. The smoke made it very hard to breathe. But he was determined not to give up. He was determined to find the animals of Gumtree Gully and do his very best to rescue them.

A few minutes later, the Ranger limped into the clearing by the creek where the animals were huddled. His hair and clothing were singed, there were burns on his arms and legs, and he was covered with scrapes and scratches from crashing through the rocks and bushes.

"Oh, I'm so glad you're here, Ranger", said Wise Old Wombat.

"What shall we do?" asked Paddle the Platypus. "Should we all get into the creek where the water can protect us?"

"No", said the Ranger as he caught his breath. "The creek isn't safe. It's far too narrow and there are tall gum trees on the other side. As soon as they start to burn, they'll crash down into the creek. The best place for us is here in this clearing."

"But—but—", squeaked young Bluey, "the clearing has thick grass and there are dead leaves all over the place—the ones you told us to clear away but we didn't. Won't the clearing burn?"

"Yes, it will", said the Ranger firmly. "It will burn. We shall burn it."

He raked together a pile of dead leaves into the centre of the clearing and set a match to the leaves. The Ranger and the animals stood back and watched the small fire he had lit burn outwards into an ever-widening circle. When it was wide enough, the Ranger beat out the small flames licking the grass with the sugar bags he carried. That left a large black circle of burnt grass. Because it had already been burned, the Ranger knew it would not burn again when the bushfire arrived.

"This is called 'back burning'", he explained to the animals. "It gives us a safe place to be while the bushfire burns around us."

Then he soaked the sugar bags in water from the creek again, and told the animals to gather right in the middle of the burnt patch and cover themselves with the wet bags.

A few minutes later, the Ranger and all the animals were huddled together under a pile of wet sugar bags, right in the centre of the burnt ground.

The bushfire got closer and the noise got louder. The heat was intense and the smoke made everyone cough and splutter. They could hear burning trees crashing down as the fire turned their trunks into ash. Some of those trees fell down over the creek—just as the Ranger had said they would.

But in the clearing there was no fire because all the grass and dead leaves had already been burned. There was nothing left in that patch for the bushfire to burn and so, at the edges of that patch of ground, the raging bushfire came to a halt.

Finally, as the afternoon wore on, the bushfire burned itself out completely. The Ranger, together with the animals of Gumtree Gully, crept out from underneath the still-damp sugar bags and looked at the ash and devastation around them.

A wind sprang up and blew away the smoke.

"Just look at that", said Rocky. "The whole gully has been burned black."

"But we are all still alive," said Wombat, "and we must be thankful for that".

"We're alive", said Bluey, "because the Ranger came into the fire and saved us".

Then Bluey turned and looked at the Ranger. He was cut and bruised, there were great burns on his arms and legs, and he looked utterly exhausted.

"It cost him a great deal of pain to save us", thought Bluey to himself. "In fact, he risked his very own life."

What's inside this story?

What the Ranger did to save the animals of Gumtree Gully is a picture of what Jesus has done to save us. And while the Ranger risked his life, Jesus actually lost his life—to save ours. The Ranger was cut, bruised and burned, but Jesus ended up with terrible scars on his hands and feet from being nailed to a cross. He died on that cross to save us.

Because he is so loving, God did something remarkable to rescue us from the punishment we deserve.

Many years ago, God sent his own Son, Jesus, into this world. Jesus never said "No" to God the way *we* all have. He always did what God wanted him to do. And so he didn't deserve to be punished like the rest of us.

But Jesus *was* punished. He was killed on a cross. God loves us so much that he punished his own Son, Jesus, *instead of us.*

This means that we can be forgiven for saying "No" to God. We can now be welcomed into God's wonderful kingdom as his friends.

The Ranger used fire (back burning) to make the animals safe from the bushfire. It is death that makes us safe from death: the death of Jesus makes us safe from "the bushfire of death" that is racing towards all of us.

The Bible says:

> God loved the world so much that he gave his only Son, so that everyone who trusts in him will have eternal life. (JOHN 3:16)

> Christ died for sins once and for all. An innocent person died for the guilty, to bring you to God. (1 PETER 3:18)

5. Out of the ashes

A TERRIFYING AND devastating bushfire had raged through Gumtree Gully. It had burned hotter than the heat of the sun and it had roared like the sound of a mighty engine. But all the animals who lived in Gumtree Gully had been saved. They had been rescued by the courage and wisdom of the Ranger.

Started by a lightning strike, the bushfire had blazed like a furnace from one end of Gumtree Gully to the other. Every tree and every bush had been scorched, blackened and burned by that fearsome fire. Not a blade of green grass was left. Everything was covered in a thick layer of sooty grey ash.

Now the animals stood beside the creek, looking at the blackened and smouldering bushland around them, glad to be alive, but sad that their beautiful home had been destroyed.

Rocky the Wallaby and Bluey the Possum went up to the Ranger and quietly thanked him for rescuing them.

"We would be dead if you hadn't come just when you did", said Rocky.

"Yes", said Bluey with tears in his big round eyes. And then, because he couldn't think of anything else to say, he said, "Thank you, Ranger". The Ranger leaned over and gently patted the possum on his furry head.

But some of the other animals had already forgotten about their rescue and were staring at the burnt and blackened bush around them.

"Just look at this mess!" sneered Sneaky the Goanna. "Now we won't be able to live here. There's not a blade of grass left—not even a green leaf on a tree! There won't be any food left for Curly or Rocky. All the fruit has been burned up, so Bluey will starve. I'll bet all the insects have been fried to a crisp too, so I'll have nothing to eat. Oh, what a mess! We're going to have to leave—all of us. We'll all have to find somewhere else to live."

A look of alarm came over Curly the Koala's face. "Without gum leaves I shall most certainly starve", he muttered in a glum voice. "Look at my favourite blue gum! It's nothing but a skeleton now—a bare, black skeleton. How can I sleep comfortably in that all day?"

Jacko the Kookaburra opened his beak and, to everyone's surprise, said, "This is no laughing matter. We have nowhere to live and nothing to eat. It's all right for me; as soon as my wing is better I can fly away. But the rest of you are in trouble." (Remember Jacko lost some feathers by bumping his wing against a tree trunk when he tried to fly away through the thick smoke of the bushfire.)

Paddle the Platypus said sadly, “Just look at my beautiful creek. It’s covered in ash and filled with burnt and broken branches. It’s as dead as a creek can be.”

“Stop being so glum, all of you”, said the Ranger. “This bushland will grow again. Everything that is black and burnt today will be bursting with greenery in just a few months. For many of these trees and plants, the ash from the fire provides fuel to grow. Just wait and see—new life shall grow out of these ashes.”

Jacko threw back his kookaburra head, opened his beak wide and began to laugh very loudly. “Now, that’s funny”, he squawked. “That’s very funny indeed. The idea that new life can grow out of such dead wood is just a hoot.” And he laughed some more.

Sneaky the Goanna joined in with a sneer saying, “What’s burnt stays burnt—everyone knows that. My Great Uncle Slither was once caught in a bushfire. He was burned to a crisp and that’s the way he stayed. Well, these trees and bushes are just as burnt as Great Uncle Slither was. And I tell you, they’ll stay burnt. Gumtree Gully will never be green again. Nothing can grow here now.”

The Ranger said quietly and seriously, “Sneaky, you are wrong. Within a few weeks, there will be green shoots and tiny leaf buds and, within a few months, you won’t recognize the place—there will be new life bursting out everywhere.”

“But what if you’re wrong?” complained Curly. “We

won't be able to stay here then. We'll have to move on and find somewhere else to live."

"But I don't want to live anywhere else", moaned Bluey.

"We like it here", added Rocky.

"This is our home", mumbled Bluey, a small tear trickling down his cheek.

"I don't think I could waddle very far," Wombat said, "not at my age".

"You won't have to move out of Gumtree Gully, I promise you", said the Ranger.

Wise Old Wombat scratched his hairy nose. "Well, I for one believe what Ranger says", he said. "If he says new life will grow out of the burnt and blackened bush, I believe him."

"So we won't have to leave?" whimpered Bluey. "Can we really stay here?"

"You won't have to leave", said the Ranger. "You can stay here in Gumtree Gully."

Jacko laughed and said, "That's all very well, but what about now? Even if these new green shoots and buds of yours do grow, it won't be for some time. What should we eat today? And tomorrow?"

"I shall bring you food", said the Ranger, "until the bushland grows back and new life appears. Until then, I shall bring in bales of hay and grasses, piles of leaves and food for all of you—even meat for you, Jacko."

"What about my creek?" asked Paddle.

"I'll pull out the biggest of the burnt branches and tree trunks, and the water will wash away all the ash", the Ranger reassured him. "And I will see to it that all of you are fed until new life and new growth springs out of all the blackness and deadness around you. You have no need to fear."

Sneaky sneered, Curly looked doubtful, and Jacko laughed out loud. "How could new life come out of a place so damaged and dead?", they all wondered.

But it turned out to be just as the Ranger had said. He brought in supplies of food for all the animals. Within a few days, rain came and washed away the worst of the ash and dust, and fed the plants and bushes with the water they needed.

Within a few weeks, tiny green buds started to appear on trees and bushes. Within a few months, there was fresh new green growth everywhere. Even the colourful wildflowers reappeared.

Within six months, it was just as lush and green as it had ever been. Gumtree Gully was a living bushland once again —just as it had been before the fire.

One day Rocky and Bluey were racing each other down the bank of the creek when Rocky suddenly stopped.

"What's the hold-up, Bigfoot?" asked Bluey. "Have you tripped over your own toes?"

"No, of course not", Rocky replied. "I'm very sure-footed. It's just that I suddenly remembered, that's all."

"Remembered what?" asked his possum friend.

"Remembered what this place was like just after the big bushfire. Now it's all grown back—just as the Ranger said it would."

Bluey looked around and said, "It's amazing stuff all right—new life, out of the ashes".

What's inside this story?

The fresh new life that grew out of the ashes in this story is a picture of what God has done with Jesus. After Jesus was killed on a cross, God brought him back to life again. God, who can make new green shoots grow out of ashes, brought Jesus alive again out of death.

Even though Jesus had really died, God brought him back to life again. Lots of people saw him and even touched him.

God, who is the source of all life, brought Jesus back to life again so that Jesus could be the bringer of new life to us.

Jesus left our world and went back to be with God, his Father. There, God made Jesus the king of the whole world.

One day, King Jesus will come back to our world. He will punish everyone who is still saying "No" to God. But at the same time, he will welcome his forgiven friends into his good kingdom forever.

The Bible says:

> God has raised Jesus to life, and taken him up to the place of honour at God's right hand.
> (ACTS 2:32-33)

> This Jesus, who was taken up into heaven, will come again in the same way as you saw him go. (ACTS 1:11)

6. The choice

A GREAT BIG BRIGHT RED waratah flower had fallen off a waratah bush. Rocky the Wallaby and Bluey the Possum were using it as a football. They had been kicking it through the dust and up and down the bushland clearing for the past hour.

At one end of the clearing, they were using two saplings—baby blue gums—as the goal posts. At the other end, two rocks were also acting as goal posts.

"Goal!" shouted Rocky as he booted the waratah flower between the two saplings. "That makes the score nine goals to nothing. Back to the middle, let's start again."

"I don't like this game", grumbled Bluey. "Those big feet of yours are built-in football boots. I want to play a game I'm good at—like hide-and-seek."

"But you always hide at the top of a tree and I can't climb trees", said Rocky. "That's not fair."

"Well, what game can we play then?" asked Bluey. "I'm not going to keep on playing footy against your big feet—that's for sure."

Before Rocky could answer, Wise Old Wombat waddled across the clearing. He was pushing a small wheelbarrow and the wheelbarrow was piled high with dead leaves.

"Of course," said Wombat as he trundled past, "you two could give up playing for a while and give me a hand with these dead leaves. Remember what the Ranger said: leaf litter is a fire hazard. We should clear up all the dead leaves so that fire doesn't have a chance in Gumtree Gully."

"Too right!" said Bluey enthusiastically. "We'll give you a hand, Wombat. Have you got another wheelbarrow or two?"

"No, but I have got two rakes that you can use to rake up the leaves for me."

"Oh, but—", complained Rocky, "can't I kick a few more goals before we go to work? Just another five or six? Or maybe seven or eight?"

"Stop putting if off, young Rocky", said Wombat sternly. "Pitch in and do your bit to help."

Reluctantly, Rocky agreed. He and Bluey collected the rakes from Wombat's burrow and set out for a part of the bush where there were heaps of dead leaves piled up against the tree trunks.

At first they raked slowly. Then Bluey said, "My pile of leaves is higher than yours".

"Oh, no it isn't", Rocky said. "I can rake faster than you."

"I'll race you", cried Bluey with a laugh and, before long, the two young friends were rushing backwards and forwards, rakes in hands, clearing paths and tracks, and heaping up leaves for Wombat to cart away, both laughing and enjoying themselves.

Jacko the Kookaburra looked down on them from high up in a river red gum. After watching them for a moment, he began to laugh. "You two do look hilarious!" he hooted. "You're like bulldozers trying to build mountains with dead leaves. Hoo! Hoo! Ha! Ha! What a joke!"

"Instead of laughing", Rocky called out, "why don't you come and give us a hand?"

"And why should I?"

"Because the Ranger says that leaf litter is a fire hazard and we don't want another bushfire in Gumtree Gully", chirped Bluey in his little possum voice.

"Oh, I see", hooted Jacko, wiping tears of laughter from his eyes. "It's a case of 'The Ranger says this' and 'The Ranger says that'. What makes you think I care what the Ranger says?"

With those words, he flew away in a feathery flutter.

Half an hour later, Wise Old Wombat, Rocky and Bluey had finished their work for the day. They had a neat pile of dead leaves right in the middle of the big clearing near the creek—right where the Ranger could burn them on the next still, calm day when there would be no wind to blow flames onto the rest of the trees and bushes.

Paddle the Platypus swam to the edge of the creek and rested his elbows on the bank. "What have you blokes been up to?" he asked.

"Clearing up the leaf litter", explained Bluey, "just like the Ranger asked us to".

Curly the Koala, looking down on them from the fork of his favourite blue gum, opened one sleepy, lazy eye and said, "Well done young fellas—keep up the good work". Then he went back to sleep again.

Sneaky the Goanna was sunning himself on a rock nearby. He looked at them over his shoulder and said, "You'd fall for anything, wouldn't you?"

"What do you mean?" asked Rocky.

"Well, it's not our job to clean up the leaf litter, is it?" sneered Sneaky. "It's the Ranger's job. He's just tricked you into doing his job for him. Of course, I'm too smart for that. No-one tricks me into anything."

"Well, if looking after Gumtree Gully—the place where we live—is not our job", said Wise Old Wombat, "what is our job? What are we here for?"

“We are here to PLAY”, shouted Paddle, doing a beautiful swan dive off a tall rock into a deep billabong. “We are here”, he said, spluttering, as he rose to the surface, “to have fun”.

“And to catch insects to eat”, sneered Sneaky, “and lie in the sun”.

Just then they heard the sound of heavy ranger boots crunching on the gravel over the bush track that led down into Gumtree Gully. They heard cheerful whistling and, a few minutes later, the tall figure of the Ranger appeared in the clearing.

“Well done!” he said, smiling when he saw the pile of dead leaves heaped up neatly in the middle of the clearing.

Rocky and Bluey beamed with pride. Wombat looked down at the ground, shuffled his feet and said, “Ah, well…”

“But I gather”, continued the Ranger, “that not everyone’s been helping”.

He looked around at the little group of animals gathered at the clearing near the creek.

“This is serious business”, continued the Ranger. “I need to know who will help. Who will follow me and care for this beautiful bushland gully? Who will sign up under my command? Will you obey me? Or will you just ignore me?”

He picked up a twig and drew a line in the dust. “I think”,

said the Ranger, "that the time has come to choose. Who will join the Ranger service under my command? And who will not? Those who wish to follow me should step across this line."

By way of reply, Jacko the Kookaburra laughed and Curly the Koala snored. Paddle the Platypus dived under the water with a splash and disappeared from view.

Sneaky the Goanna called out, "No-one tells me what to do—not even a Ranger". He scuttled off under a rock.

Wise Old Wombat stepped across the line and said, "You are the Ranger—you are our Rescuer and our Ruler".

Rocky and Bluey stepped across the line and stood beside Wombat.

The Ranger looked around and said, "Well then, everyone has made their choice. Do the rest of you really want to stay on your side of the line?"

Four voices came in a chorus of replies:

"Sure!"

"I belong on this side of the line!"

"Me too!"

"I'm not shifting!"

Then a very serious and grave expression came across the Ranger's face as he said, "Where the line in the dust is, that's where I'll build the wire fence".

"Fence? What fence?" spluttered Paddle.

"You didn't tell us there was going to be a fence", Sneaky yelled, without coming out from underneath his rock.

"This side of the fence—the larger end of Gumtree Gully—will be cared for by me and my workers. The rebels who won't work can live on the other side of the fence—in the narrow end of the gully. The wire fence will run through the creek as well as over the rocks. It will fully enclose the narrow end of the gully, like a big aviary or cage at the zoo. That will stop you making a mess of anywhere else."

"But that end", protested Curly, "is mainly rocks".

"And the creek is shallow there", Paddle complained.

"And there aren't very many trees", moaned Jacko—who didn't feel like laughing any more.

"I don't care", snarled Sneaky. "I'd rather lie about on rocks than work for the Ranger."

"I care", groaned Curly. "I didn't realize there'd be... consequences."

Wise Old Wombat looked at Curly and said, "Did you really think you could get away with ignoring the Ranger forever? Intelligent animals like you must have worked out that your actions would have consequences... sooner or later."

What's inside this story?

The choice the Ranger offered the animals in this story is a picture of the choice God offers us. We can either step across the line to follow Jesus, serve him and please God, or we can keep on saying "No" to God.

There are many people who keep on saying "No" to God and who keep on pretending to be their own king. But all who do these things will be punished by God and shut out of his good kingdom forever.

You can step across the line. You can say "Sorry" to God. You can start living with Jesus as your king and enjoy being in God's kingdom forever. You can be like the wise animals in the story. They chose to step across the line and sign up in the Ranger's service. They recognized that the Ranger was both their Rescuer and Ruler. They promised to obey and serve him.

Jesus wants us to do the same. We can sign up to be in *Jesus'* service under *Jesus'* command, recognizing him as our Rescuer and Ruler and promising to obey and serve him.

There are really only two ways to live:

The first way is to keep saying "No" to God, pretending to be your own king. But if you do that, you won't win, because God is God. God will shut you out of his kingdom forever.

The second way is to stop saying "No" to God and to ask God to forgive you. God *will* forgive you and welcome you as his friend. Because Jesus died to take your punishment, God promises that he won't be angry with you any more.

You can then start living with God's Son, Jesus, as your King, doing whatever he wants you to do. You can look forward to being in God's good kingdom forever.

You can step across the line and say "Yes" to God by saying *sorry, thanks* and *please:* saying **sorry** for not treating God as your king; saying **thanks** for sending Jesus to die so that you can be forgiven; and asking him to **please** forgive you, change you and help you live with Jesus as your king, both now and forever.

So who will be *your* king?

The Bible says:

> Everyone who trusts in the Son has eternal life. But everyone who rejects him will never share in that life. (JOHN 3:36)

Things for adults to talk about with kids

Gumtree Gully and 'Two Ways to Live'

The story of *Gumtree Gully* is loosely based on the gospel outline *Two Ways to Live*, and in particular on the children's version of the outline, called *Who will be King?*

Each of the six chapters of *Gumtree Gully* touches on one of the six points of the *Two Ways to Live* outline, namely:

- God's creation of the world, his ownership of the world, and his claim on us.
- Our rebellion against God's good rule, and our desire to do things our own way.
- God's judgement against our rebellion.
- God's love in sending his Son to die in our place to take our punishment upon himself.
- The resurrection of Jesus to new life, as the ruler and life-giver.
- The choice that we all face.

Like all allegorical tales, the correspondence between the

story and the truths it is illustrating is not exact, and we shouldn't try to make it so. The story illustrates the six main points in a general way and (hopefully) helps young readers grasp the ideas. The 'What's in this story?' section at the end of each chapter points out the connections between the story of *Gumtree Gully* and the Christian gospel. If you're reading or discussing the story with a child, you can use the questions and suggestions below as a further resource.

1. The Ranger

What this story is all about: **God's creation**.

> Our Lord and God, you are worthy to receive glory, honour and power, because you created all things, and by your decision they came to be. (REVELATION 4:11)

- Why should we honour (respect) and praise God?
- Is there anything in creation that does not depend on God?
- What attitude should people have to a God like this?

2. The animals

What this story is all about: **Our rebellion**.

> No-one is acceptable to God. No-one understands or searches for God. They have all turned away. (ROMANS 3:10-12)

- Have we human beings done a good job of running our world and ourselves?
- How many people are acceptable to God (living exactly the way he wants them to)?
- How many people really search for God, to be his friend?
- How many people have turned away from God's rule and said "No" to him?

3. The bushfire

What this story is all about: **God's judgement**.

> We will all die once, and then face judgement. (HEBREWS 9:27)

- What two things will happen to every person?
- What must everyone face after death?

4. The rescue

What this story is all about: **God's love**.

> Christ died for sins once and for all. An innocent person died for the guilty, to bring you to God. (1 PETER 3:18)

- Why did Jesus Christ die?
- Who is the innocent person mentioned here?
- Who are the guilty people?
- Which of these two words—'guilty' or 'innocent'—describes you?

- What can Jesus' death do for you?

5. Out of the ashes

What this story is all about: **God's power.**

> God has raised Jesus to life, and taken him up to the place of honour at God's right hand. (ACTS 2:32-33)

> This Jesus, who was taken up into heaven, will come again in the same way as you saw him go. (ACTS 1:11)

- What has God done for Jesus?
- What will Jesus do in the future? Why?

6. The choice

What this story is all about: **Our challenge.**

> Everyone who trusts in the Son has eternal life. But everyone who rejects him will never share in that life. (JOHN 3:36)

- What two types of people are described here?
- What must you do to have eternal life (live in God's kingdom forever)?
- Why will some people never share in eternal life?
- Which of these two ways is the way *you* want to live?

Two Ways to Live

Two Ways to Live is a clearly written, six-point presentation of what the average non-Christian person needs to understand to become a Christian. The six points provide a brief summary of the whole Bible, with simple diagrams to illustrate the ideas.

Matthias Media publishes a range of *Two Ways to Live* resources to suit different purposes. These resources include a tract, a Bible study, and a training course designed to help every Christian know and understand the gospel clearly for themselves, and be able to explain their faith effectively when the opportunity arises. For information about these resources, visit: **www.twowaystolive.com**

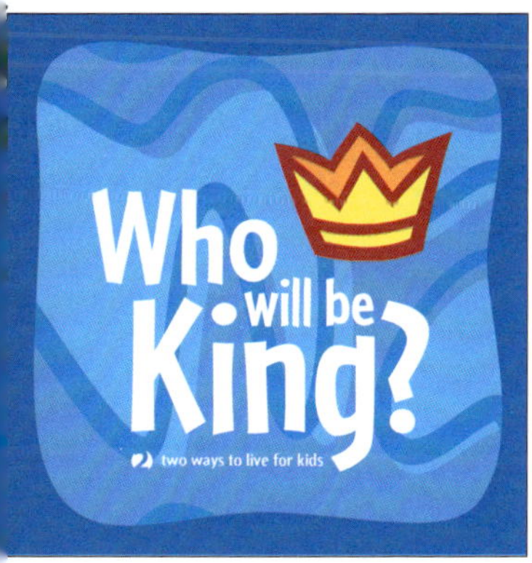

Carefully written and illustrated for young readers (roughly ages 7-11), *Who Will be King?* is a presentation of the gospel based on the *Two Ways to Live* outline and illustrations. With simple, clear language, but concern for the sensitivity of younger children, it is ideal for Scripture teaching, Sunday School classes, beach missions, camps, or just for giving to young friends and family members. It can also form the basis of a short Bible time with children, focusing on one point each day. More information about how to use *Who Will be King?* can be found on the *Two Ways to Live* website.